What Needs the Sun

David Bauer

Rigby

A Harcourt Achieve Imprint

www.Rigby.com
1-800-531-5015

Here is a flower.
It needs the sun.

Here is a plant.
It needs the sun.

Here is a forest.

It needs the sun.

Here is a cat.
It needs the sun.

Here is a lizard.
It needs the sun.

Here is a snake.
It needs the sun.

Here is a frog.

It needs the sun.

Here is a bat.

Does it need the sun?